THE ENI[OF J. ED[HOOVER

Biography, Authority, Ambiguity, and the Legacy of Law Enforcement

MacVix Publishers

CONTENTS

PREAMBLE

When we look at the embroidery of American history, one figure stands out as truly remarkable — John Edgar Hoover. A man whose story is truly remarkable, showcasing the unwavering dedication and profound influence that has left an indelible mark on the field of law enforcement in the United States.

John Edgar Hoover served as the first Director of the Federal Bureau of Investigation (FBI) and his influence was significant from 1924 until his death in 1972.

Hoover took on the responsibility of leading the Bureau of Investigation in 1924, which later became the FBI. He played a crucial part in establishing the FBI in 1935 and continued to be a guiding force for an impressive 37 years until he passed away at the age of 77.

And now, Hoover's impact goes far beyond his own era, leaving a lasting imprint on technological advancements. His indelible influence can be seen in the centralized fingerprint archives and pioneering forensic laboratories. Under his leadership, the FBI's reach expanded and it transformed into a powerful force in the fight against crime, surpassing its initial capabilities.

However, there were shadows that danced alongside his amazing accomplishments. Hoover was responsible for overseeing the development of a nationwide blacklist, which became widely known as the FBI Index - a file with secrets about many public figures, which could potentially ruin their reputations – who knows?

It's interesting how history reveals a paradox. There have been whispers that

Hoover, despite his polished public image, had a hidden life in the subculture of homosexual transvestism. It is said that organized crime possessed this knowledge, which was a powerful tool that influenced Hoover's actions. They tried to distract him from their own actions by urging him to focus his efforts on unsuspecting targets. He focused his attention on influential figures such as Charles Chaplin, known for his liberal views, and Martin Luther King, a prominent advocate for civil rights. It seems that even the most influential individuals can still be affected by unexpected events.

Hoover's deliberate refusal to acknowledge the existence of a nationwide organized crime syndicate eventually fell apart, much to everyone's surprise. In the early 1960s, Mafia assassin Joe Valachi made a confession before Congress. This confession finally made Hoover acknowledge a reality that he had been resisting for years.

This story only provides the extensive life of John Edgar Hoover. Within them is a deeper comprehension of the man who greatly influenced the direction of law enforcement with an unforgettable impact.

CHAPTER ONE

THE EARLY YEARS OF J. EDGAR HOOVER'S LIFE

HERITAGE

Hoover's family history had connections to both Maryland and Pennsylvania, which played a significant role in the unfolding story. However, the complexities of this historical puzzle created a mysterious tapestry, where strands of identity were interwoven.

John Edgar Hoover's family can be traced back to Swiss-German roots. His father's side of the family came from

Switzerland, and the last name "Hoover" has Swiss-German roots. In Switzerland, the name was originally spelled "Huber" before his ancestors moved to the United States and it was changed to "Hoover" to fit the English language.

It is likely that the Huber/Hoover family immigrated to the United States a few generations before John Edgar Hoover was born. The Swiss-German heritage indicates a family background that has connections to both Switzerland and the German-speaking areas of Europe. Unfortunately, there isn't much information publicly available about the Hoover family's ancestral journey and the generations that preceded John Edgar Hoover.

It's worth mentioning that although family heritage and ancestry can give us a glimpse into someone's background and cultural influences, John Edgar Hoover's public reputation was mostly shaped by his position as the first Director of the FBI and his influence on American law enforcement and intelligence.

Hoover had a fairly typical upbringing for that era, growing up in a household that placed a strong emphasis on education and discipline. He attended Central High School in Washington, D.C., and showed an early interest in law and government. His interest eventually led him to study law at George Washington University, and he successfully graduated with a law degree in 1917.

Although Hoover's family background may not have had a noticeable impact on his career or actions as the director of the FBI, it is likely that his upbringing and education influenced his values, ambitions, and professional approach. However, it is his own accomplishments that ultimately define his public legacy.

EARLY BEGINNINGS AND CHILDHOOD DAYS

In the context of his family heritage, we've seen how the story of John Edgar Hoover began as a man shaped by a beautiful blend of heritage, politics, and ambition, creating a symphony that would resonate throughout history. Now, let's go back to January 1, 1895, where the story of John Edgar Hoover's beginnings specifically started.

He was born into this world as a child of destiny, with his parents being Dickerson Naylor Hoover and Annie Marie Scheitlin Hoover. Both of them were committed public servants working for the United States Government.

Young Hoover grew up in a neighborhood just three blocks away from Capitol Hill, the center of political activity, in the lively city of Washington, D.C. A place that was deeply influenced by the rhythms of governance. Throughout his family's history, a legacy was created through their involvement in government service. Hoover's journey was guided by this legacy, which was like a compass. It was a journey where politics and governance were deeply ingrained in him.

In this family setting, his father, who was a member of the Coast Guard, served as a shining example of unwavering dedication. Hoover was not the only star in the family's lineage. He had two siblings who also shared the sky with him. His younger sister was named Lillian Margaret and his older brother was named Dickerson Naylor Jr.

However, in the midst of all the collective dreams at home, their family's story was not without its fair share of challenges. Hoover's life took a difficult turn when his father unexpectedly left when he was just seven years old. This left their strong-willed mother to navigate the challenges of raising their family on her own. The relationship between Hoover and his mother, Annie, gave birth to a fragile connection that brought intimacy to his early life. The time they shared was special, a time when their unique relationship could thrive. It held precious memories that he treasured and needed to thrive as a youngster, providing comfort as he maneuvered through the challenges of the outside world.

During these young days, Hoover showed a strong and determined spirit, which played a significant role in shaping his successful journey. He was already a smart thinker; he was already nicknamed "Speed" because it represented his fast-paced way of speaking, which was a clear reflection of his sharp mind. He decided to join the debate team in his high school because he wanted to overcome his struggle with stuttering.

EDUCATIONAL FOUNDATION OF JOHN EDGAR HOOVER

John Edgar Hoover showed a keen interest in law from a young age and was highly committed to his studies throughout his educational journey. He went to Central High School in Washington, D.C., and was known for being a hardworking and academically focused student. While he was there, he started to become interested in law and government.

Hoover continued his education at George Washington University after completing high school and his presence there brought light to the darkness of his early world. It was at this school that he began a journey of learning that would greatly influence his future. He studied hard and was known for his dedication and disciplined work ethic while pursuing a Bachelor of Laws degree. He kept doing really well in his academics and showed a lot of discipline in how he approached his studies, then, became involved in legal topics that would later be very important for his career In law enforcement.

Finally, he graduated with his law degree from George Washington University in 1917 – a strong education that equipped him with a solid understanding of legal principles, research skills, and critical thinking abilities. John Edgar Hoover's experiences in school, especially during his time at George Washington University, played a significant role in shaping his future accomplishments in the fields of law enforcement and intelligence.

CHAPTER TWO

THE MAJOR MILESTONES IN HOOVER'S CAREER

Well, attending George Washington University and becoming familiar with the legal and governmental scene in Washington, D.C., was able to build a strong foundation for his impressive rise in the law enforcement field. With this spirit, he started his career by taking on different positions in the Department of Justice. During this time, he used his legal expertise to work on issues concerning national security and law enforcement.

DESTINED PATHS: THE DEPARTMENT OF JUSTICE, RISE TO POWER AND LEADERSHIP

A journey filled with meaning and strength: Hoover's life was touched by a significant moment during a time of great historical change. In 1917, the United States was caught up in the midst of World War I. However, despite the urging to take action, Hoover's future took a different path. There was a strategic position in the Justice Department that he found, which allowed him to avoid military service.

This place of refuge was a clear indication of his distinct journey. People in positions of influence were already talking about his abilities and his conservative beliefs could be heard throughout the halls of power. During the chaotic time of war, Attorney General A. Mitchell Palmer noticed Hoover with a careful eye. Palmer was drawn to Hoover's competence, and he was quickly given the leadership role of the General Intelligence Division (GID). The GID was created to protect against extremist organizations and was a powerful force.

The year 1919 was filled with great significance. It was a time when the GID spread its influence, carrying out raids that had a lasting impact on history. As the GID cast its net, hundreds of people suspected of affiliations with radical factions were ensnared, making search warrants seem like mere formalities. This chapter, which is commonly referred to as the "Palmer Raids," was orchestrated by J. Edgar Hoover. He secretly planned and carried out actions to deport people who were accused of engaging in subversive activities.

However, in the midst of all the planning and coordination, the story took an unexpected turn. The person behind these operations, A. Mitchell Palmer, was a prominent figure in politics, but his path was hindered by the chaotic response that followed. His career was overshadowed by the aftermath, causing him to retire due to the negative impact. Despite the whirlwind of change, Hoover managed to emerge unscathed, with his reputation remaining untarnished.

The story later continued to unfold, taking us to the year 1924. President

Calvin Coolidge made a bold move that will forever be remembered in history. In his complex web of choices, he selected the young Hoover, who was only 29 years old, for a highly significant position - the directorship of the Bureau of Investigation (BI). Hoover had longed for this position for a considerable amount of time, with a deep desire that was ingrained in his very being.

As the tides changed, Hoover's vision became a requirement for acceptance. There was a strong message that echoed out - the bureau's independence, free from political influence, and the director's loyalty only to the attorney general. The condition was defined by its strong commitment to integrity and the relentless pursuit of pure justice.

So, in his early career, Hoover's journey took place during a time of intense war, political unrest, and his own strong beliefs. His journey, from being exempted to gaining power, was filled with determination and direction. Every step taken led to the rise of a man who would make a lasting impact on the course of history.

INSIDE BI: HOOVER'S EPOCH OF CHANGE AND JUSTICE

During his time as director, Hoover's influence was evident in the policies that were implemented. He managed the institution with great skill and his actions had a significant impact. He had the ability to let go of people he believed were only in their positions due to political connections or lacked the necessary qualifications, all in his quest for excellence. The pursuit of quality didn't end with recruitment; it extended into a thorough process. The new agent candidates were taken through a series of background checks, interviews that went beyond the surface, and demanding physical assessments.

Hoover's influence as a financial maestro reverberated through the halls of Congress. His strategic acumen was evident as funds surged forward. In the midst of these impressive financial achievements, a laboratory appeared, serving as a symbol of the harmonious blend of science and justice. In his time, data was being processed in a systematic and scientific manner. It was collected with great care and analyzed with meticulous attention to detail.

THE METAMORPHOSIS TO FBI

Throughout American history, there was a significant change in the way law enforcement and national security were approached. This transformation was marked by the use of initials, which symbolized the beginning of a new era. The transition from BI to FBI was an incredible transformation that took place in a world that was constantly changing.

As time passed and history unfolded, significant changes began to take shape.

The Bureau of Investigation (BI) was like a guardian in the halls of power, always there to ensure justice was upheld. Its mission was deeply ingrained in its very essence. However, a new era was on the horizon, and in 1935, a new chapter began.

A significant decision was made in the chambers of Congress - the creation of the Federal Bureau of Investigation (FBI). This marked a significant change in purpose, where it adopted a new identity that embraced a wider mission of protecting the nation from threats both inside and outside its borders. J. Edgar Hoover, a symbol of unwavering dedication, took on the role of leadership as a fresh mantle was given to him. He carried the weight of leadership on his shoulders, and he wore it with pride until he retired in 1972.

The metamorphosis symbolized a commitment to change, to overcome the limitations of the past, and to embody a vibrant energy that resonated with the needs of the present and future.

The change wasn't just about words; it was a complete transformation that reflected the evolving world around us. The initials "BI" were expanded to "FBI" to represent a dedication to strengthening the country's security system and being able to adapt and respond effectively to new challenges. The FBI became a strong and powerful organization, capable of tackling not just regular crime but also handling the challenges of espionage, counterintelligence, and international threats.

However, even during significant historical events, there were challenges that affected the heartland. During the 1930s, the Midwest experienced a period of intense fear and violence caused by ruthless gangsters. They used their arsenal of weapons and fast getaway vehicles to control smaller communities, making it impossible for local law enforcement to stop them. At the same time, criminal organizations that operate across multiple cities have a significant influence on metropolitan areas. Hoover's advocacy proved successful in this chaotic situation. The Bureau's agents were given authority to confront these criminal syndicates that had the audacity to break federal interstate laws.

Legends such as John Dillinger and the notorious "Machine Gun" Kelly experienced the relentless pursuit of justice. This was a dance that took place, involving pursuit, capture, trial, and in certain situations, execution. The Bureau's strong presence in the minds of Americans gave rise to a nickname, "G-men," which symbolized justice and duty.

As the shadows of World War II approached, the FBI transformed into a guardian of national defense. A new battlefront emerged, one that involves fighting against the encroachment of Nazis and Communists within the intelligence community. Hoover's agents assumed the responsibility of internal counterintelligence, demonstrating a watchfulness that safeguarded the nation from threats within its own borders.

Moreover, President Franklin D. Roosevelt also had a big task for the FBI. He wanted them to gather intelligence from all over the Western Hemisphere, which was a huge job. Even in the middle of this complex situation, criminal activities continued to occur and influence the overall picture. The world of heists, kidnappings, and car thefts is always present, leaving its mark. However, despite these challenges, Hoover and his bureau managed to maintain their unwavering commitment to transformation, serving as a symbol of justice in a world that was constantly evolving.

EPOCH OF TENSIONS: HOOVER'S UNFOLDING BATTLE AGAINST SUBVERSION

During the tense era of the Cold War, J. Edgar Hoover emerged as a powerful figure, displaying unwavering determination fueled by strong beliefs that shone brightly, much like a guiding star. During that time, different ideologies clashed, creating a sort of battleground where people were strongly against communism and feared the possibility of subversion. In the midst of all the chaos, Hoover became determined and developed a comprehensive strategy, which eventually led to the creation of the well-known Counter Intelligence Programme, also known as COINTELPRO.

As the Cold War intensified, Hoover's personal opposition to Communism and subversion grew stronger. He was a strategic visionary who understood the constraints holding back the investigative division of the Justice Department. So, they came up with COINTELPRO, a series of secret actions meant to influence the outcome against radical political groups.

The operations of COINTELPRO were kept secret, filled with surveillance and intrigue. Numerous undercover investigations, some of which pushed the limits of legality, formed a compelling narrative. The objective had two parts: to damage the reputation of radical organizations and to disrupt their operations. Originally, it was created to counter foreign agents trying to infiltrate the government. However, it quickly transformed into a tool that Hoover used to target any group or individual involved in activities he considered to be subversive.

The targets varied greatly, representing a wide range of ideologies. COINTELPRO kept a close eye on the Ku Klux Klan, the Socialist Workers Party, and the Black Panthers, and recognized their significance and potential threats. However, out of all the different portrayals in this mosaic, the one that was the most chilling was the one of Martin Luther King Jr. He was labeled as the most dangerous Negro in the future of the nation. As a result, he was subjected to constant surveillance, with every action carefully recorded and his private conversations secretly captured.

Hoover was relentless in his search for weaknesses in King's armor. Whispers filled the air, swirling with allegations of Communist ties and unseemly behavior. Hoover's toolkit was incredibly sneaky, including illegal wiretaps that invaded people's privacy by listening in on their conversations, and searches without a warrant that pushed the limits of what was legal.

In 1971, something significant happened that marked a turning point. The curtain of secrecy was lifted, revealing the inner workings of COINTELPRO to the public.

The revelations were quite impactful, revealing not just the actions of the FBI but also shedding light on the actions of other institutions. The Central Intelligence Agency (CIA) became part of the story by getting involved in activities like infiltration, burglary, unlawful wiretapping, planting evidence, and spreading made-up rumors to suppress dissent.

Even though there was a lot of criticism and backlash directed towards Hoover and the FBI, he continued to be a strong and determined leader. He held his position until the very end of his life, and it only came to an end when he passed away.

Hoover's legacy in the annals of history is a fascinating blend of ideals centered around protection and the less visible aspects of power. His actions resonate throughout history, serving as a reminder of the delicate balance between security and freedom during a time characterized by passion and apprehension.

THE COMPLEX LEGACY

J. Edgar Hoover played a significant role in shaping the Federal Bureau of Investigation (FBI) throughout history. His personal ideals were deeply ingrained in the organization, making him a master artisan in the grand embroidery of its development. His beliefs were intricately interwoven with the contours of discipline and patriotism, which were clearly evident in the essence of the organization.

However, as power and influence grew, a mysterious duality began to emerge. During Hoover's time as the head of the

FBI, the organization engaged in secret surveillance within the United States, which involved activities that raised ethical concerns. He summoned justifications, rooted in his conservative patriotism and the whispers of paranoia that echoed in his mind.

For many years, people have been talking about his unconventional methods behind closed doors in positions of authority. He was covered in a cloak of suspicion, carefully crafted by government authorities who were trying to understand the extent of his actions.

However, he had a certain air of popularity surrounding him, which acted as a protective barrier that even presidents from Truman to Nixon were reluctant to challenge. They were acutely aware of the political consequences, which heavily influenced their decision-making process.

Afterwards, the Church Committee came into existence, aiming to reflect on and shed light on the situation. Senator Frank Church, who was a guiding light in this pursuit, was the chairperson of the committee that was named after him. In

1975, there was a significant investigation that shed light on the secretive operations of COINTELPRO. It was like a symphony of inquiry, revealing the hidden aspects of their activities. The committee's findings were truly remarkable. They uncovered numerous instances of illegal activities and, in many cases, a violation of the fundamental principles that unite our nation.

Hoover's transformation of the FBI left behind a complex legacy that encompassed both discipline and surveillance, as well as elements of patriotism and overreach. In his actions, he carefully navigated the fine line between seeking justice and protecting freedom. His story is now etched within the pages of history, a captivating exploration of power and its lingering effects that still resonate throughout the passage of time.

CHAPTER THREE

HOOVER'S TENURE AS FBI DIRECTOR: A SUMMARY OF CONTROVERSIES

BLACKMAIL AND INTIMIDATION

There have been claims that Hoover used the information he obtained through surveillance to blackmail and intimidate people, including politicians, celebrities, and public figures. This situation caused a sense of fear and vulnerability, which gave him the ability to exert excessive control over numerous influential individuals.

COINTELPRO

It's also believed by many that the FBI's COINTELPRO operations were focused on different political groups with the goal of disrupting and neutralizing them. The program used various strategies like spreading false information, creating conflicts within organizations, and even encouraging violence. COINTELPRO targeted civil rights groups, anti-war activists, and leftist organizations. Critics claim that these operations went beyond the scope of maintaining law and order, and instead, they eroded the democratic rights of citizens to express their dissenting opinions.

DOMESTIC SURVEILLANCE

The FBI, under Hoover's leadership, carried out widespread surveillance on American citizens within the country, often without obtaining the necessary legal authorization. They engaged in activities such as wiretapping, infiltrating organizations, and gathering information about people's personal lives. One of the most significant examples is when Hoover targeted civil rights leaders, anti-war activists, and political dissidents. The surveillance has caused a lot of worry because it seems to be infringing on people's privacy and their rights to freedom of speech.

HOOVER'S OWN IMAGE

Hoover was quite adept at using the media to portray himself as a national hero and the FBI as an institution that could do no wrong. He was very deliberate in how he presented himself to the public, making sure to divert attention from any controversies and project an image of unquestionable authority.

To sum it up, John Edgar Hoover's legacy is a mix of achievements in modernizing law enforcement and intelligence, but also tainted by controversies surrounding civil liberties violations, abuse of power, and political manipulation. These controversies bring attention to the complicated and sometimes troublesome aspects of his leadership. They also spark conversations about the ethical limits of law enforcement in a democratic society.

LACK OF DIVERSITY

During his time as the head of the FBI, Hoover was resistant to the idea of diversifying the agency's personnel. This meant that there were limited opportunities for women and minority agents to join the organization. The agency's inability to have a diverse workforce made it difficult for them to effectively meet the needs of a diverse society and also led to systemic biases.

PERSONAL VENDETTAS

Hoover's actions were influenced by his personal grudges against people he saw as enemies. He misused the resources of the FBI to go after people he had personal issues with, which often led to unfounded investigations and harm to their reputation. The FBI's impartiality was undermined due to the misuse of federal power, which resulted in a loss of trust.

POLITICAL MANIPULATION

Hoover collected a lot of information on politicians, whether they were in power or not, in order to have influence over them. He utilized this information to shape political decisions, manipulate elections, and maintain his own power. The manipulation of political figures has made it difficult to distinguish between law enforcement and political control.

THE CIVIL RIGHTS MOVEMENT

The FBI did conduct investigations into civil rights violations, but Hoover's views on racial equality were quite controversial. At first, he was hesitant to acknowledge and tackle the issue of systemic racism within the FBI. He also showed resistance to the idea of investigating civil rights cases. In addition, he also authorized the surveillance of Martin Luther King Jr. These actions went against the idea of fair law enforcement and made people question if there was any personal bias involved.

THE MISUSE OF POWER

Some critics believe that Hoover's leadership style was authoritarian, which resulted in a culture of secrecy. They argue that dissent was suppressed and there was a lack of accountability. He used his position to protect the Bureau from being monitored and questioned, which resulted in a lack of systems in place to ensure accountability.

CHAPTER FOUR

PERSONAL LIFE OF J. EDGAR HOOVER

J. EDGAR HOOVER AND CLYDE TOLSON

Clyde Tolson was a person who had a close relationship with John Edgar Hoover, who was the Director of the Federal Bureau of Investigation (FBI) for a long time. Tolson was not only an associate but also a trusted friend of Hoover. Many historians and researchers have speculated and discussed the nature of Tolson's relationship with Hoover. Some suggest that they had a close personal connection that went beyond their professional ties.

Hoover and Tolson met in the late 1920s, brought together by fate's tender embrace. Maybe, although the exact details have become less clear over time, it happened at the famous bar of the Mayflower Hotel. There was a mysterious thread of destiny that brought them together, connecting Tolson to the group of dashing young men from the George Washington fraternity. Hoover's orbit attracted these vibrant stars during his early days as the director of the FBI, starting in 1928.

Clyde Tolson worked closely with Hoover for many years as the Associate Director of the FBI. He had an important position in the organization, and his job involved overseeing administrative and operational tasks. Tolson and Hoover had a strong bond both professionally and personally. They were not only close friends but also worked closely together.

Although there is plenty of evidence of their professional collaboration, people have been speculating about the nature of their personal relationships for some time now. There are differing opinions among historians and biographers regarding the nature of Hoover and Tolson's relationship. Some argue that they were romantically involved, while others believe that they had a deep and close friendship that was not romantic in nature. Maybe that can be left for them to answer since the historical evidence does not provide a clear answer.

No matter what kind of relationship they had, it's obvious that Clyde Tolson played a significant role in John Edgar

Hoover's life. He was someone they could trust and rely on, not just as an advisor, but also as a companion and colleague. Their bond had a profound effect on their personal lives and their positions within the FBI. Tolson stayed loyal to Hoover until Hoover passed away in 1972, and Tolson himself died in 1975.

Tolson's career as an agent soared quickly and effortlessly, thanks to his exceptional abilities. By 1931, he had worked his way up in the Bureau and was now known as the assistant director. The hands of the clock moved as if they were dancing. His role was not insignificant; it carried the weight of enforcing Hoover's well-known attention to detail.

In the early days of the Bureau, it was quite common for people to quickly rise through the ranks. Hoover had a keen eye for talent and would identify individuals he believed had great potential. He would then help them rise through the ranks of the Bureau, reaching the highest levels of the organization. Tolson became a central figure in the story, not just because of his skills, but also because of the deep connection that formed between him and his employer.

As the 1930s unfolded, Tolson became a constant presence by Hoover's side, accompanying him to important events in Washington, D.C. Their camaraderie was a vital part of these moments, from the lively echoes of Bureau baseball games to the prestigious gatherings at the White House. It was a bond that truly enriched these experiences. Their journey went beyond the boundaries of the District, without being limited by geographical constraints. The FBI's reputation resounded as they chased after kidnappers and bank robbers, ultimately bringing them to the bustling streets of New York City. They went to the prestigious Stork Club, where they had the pleasure of being in the presence of famous figures like Damon Runyon and Jack Dempsey. They experienced the echoes of history when they found themselves in the press section alongside Winchell at a Dempsey fight in 1935. It was a memorable night that perfectly captured the spirit of that time.

Hoover and Tolson's bond formed in the captivating interplay of history and humanity. Throughout their journey together, they experienced both gentle and challenging moments that left a lasting impression on their lives.

Today, the stories from history only give us a glimpse into the mysterious bond that developed between J. Edgar Hoover and Clyde Tolson. The bits of information from the public domain shed an interesting light on how they are connected. When we look at their documented interactions, we catch a glimpse of the intricate threads of their companionship. These threads are filled with subtle nuances that are not easily understood. However, once the veil of privacy is removed, what we are left with is a landscape filled with speculation. Journalists and historians have been eagerly trying to uncover the true nature of Hoover and Tolson's relationship, but there is still a lot of uncertainty surrounding it.

So the question remains: in what way did their bond manifest? Dustin Lance Black, the talented writer of the television series "J. Edgar," used his artistic skills to create a powerful and emotional story. He saw their relationship as a solemn foreshadowing of the current landscape of legal partnerships. In the story, the focus was on their personal conflicts - intense arguments around a table filled with food, and the turbulent emotions that the main character experienced.

However, it is interesting to note that the parts of their story that are visible to the public, the aspects that are known by everyone, tend to be the most captivating pieces. Their relationship was surrounded by an air of secrecy, as they never openly acknowledged the romantic or sexual aspect of their connection. Yet, within this shroud of silence, there existed a complexity that challenged the societal norms of their time.

Their story is one that involves two souls deeply connected, a bond that cannot be easily categorized. The dance between Hoover and Tolson, painted with the brushstrokes of companionship, resonates throughout history. The intertwining of emotions, like a beautiful tapestry, creates a heartfelt plea for you to stay with me always.

CHARITABLE LEGACY OF J. EDGER HOOVER

Nurturing Futures

It is commonly known that the J. Edgar Hoover Foundation shines a sympathetic light on aspirant students dipping their toes into the world of forensic science.

This charitable non-profit organization was founded in 1965 as a result of the vision of former special agents and other people who shared the goal of promoting J. Edgar Hoover's ideals. With unwavering commitment, the Foundation has awarded more than $3.5 million in scholarships to deserving students around the country who have aspirations to pursue careers in forensic science or law enforcement studies.

But the Foundation's impact goes beyond just providing financial support; it also issues a passionate invitation to others to take up the noble cause and carry on J. Edgar Hoover's legacy of advancing forensic science education. Students at West Virginia University have reason to be hopeful, especially those enrolled in the Eberly College of Arts and Sciences' Department of Forensic and Investigative Science. The J. Edgar Hoover Foundation Leadership Scholarship, which was offered to the institution in 2016, offers up a path to aspire in this situation.

The Hoover Foundation stretched its charitable arms throughout the academic year 2016–2017, ushering in a magnificent chapter that lived up to the foundation's philanthropic ideals. Four worthy kids received scholarships as a result of this one extraordinary act. These lucky students, who were either juniors or seniors, started on a path to academic success and financial security. Evidence of financial need, a hint of leadership ability, and an academic record with a minimum grade point average of 3.3 were the marks of merit that decorated the eligibility mantle.

Gerald Lang, the eminent figurehead of the Department of Forensic and Investigative Science, said that this organization was laying out the future of the discipline. He mentioned how students from 31 different states came together here to shape their futures, which is evidence of the program's rising national reputation. A gift from the Hoover Foundation, an expression of national respect created for its researchers, gave the Department's body of knowledge a striking stroke of recognition.

In addition to receiving financial assistance, each scholarship winner received the prestigious designation of Hoover Scholar, which gave their resumes a dazzling sheen and improved their chances for success outside of the exclusive walls of academia. The partnership with the J. Edgar Hoover Foundation became more significant as the Department of Forensic and Investigative Science broadened its needlepoint and created new opportunities for its students. A tangible synergy emerged, building a connection between ambitions and the FBI's

Criminal Justice Information Services Division in Clarksburg, West Virginia. This bridge will provide students with a variety of internships, field experiences, and post-graduation options.

The 2016–2017 school year saw the honorees Morgan Abbott, Darby Stemple, Tabetha Soberdash, and Micayla Zynda revel in the glory of their selection. Their experiences as teaching assistants, members of famous national honor societies, and sincere volunteer activities that reverberated across the community left traces of leadership in their tales. Their pursuit of success in the revered halls of academia was complimented by traits that exemplify leadership and citizenship, crafting a tapestry of opportunity for others to follow.

THE TRAGIC DEPARTURE OF J. EDGAR

On May 2, 1972, J. Edgar Hoover's time on earth came to an end in the peaceful embrace of the night. His gentle death was brought on by the signs of high blood pressure, a condition that had been looming over him. J. Edgar Hoover passed away at the venerable age of 77 in the sanctity of his bedroom. Hoover, an icon of steadfast dominance over the FBI, just finished a long day's work at his office the previous day. At 8:30 in the morning, his dedicated maid made the heartbreaking discovery - the once a symbol of authority was now peacefully lying face down near his bed on the floor.

The cause of death was given by the distinguished Dr. James L. Luke, Chief Medical Examiner for the State of Washington: "hypertensive cardiovascular disease." The sickness had been present inside the walls of his heart, but its specifics were obscured. His life's delicate threads had created a tapestry, but one thread was broken—possibly the heart, which had become weary from too much stress. However, Dr. Luke said that there would be no need for an autopsy since his death was a natural acceptance of the hereafter.

Acting Attorney General Richard G. Kleindienst served as the messenger of the grim news to FBI offices across the globe at 11 a.m. Congress promptly approved Hoover's body's resting place in the revered Capitol Rotunda after realizing that a giant had fallen; only 21 other souls, including presidents and statesmen, had ever received this honor. Hoover's body was moved to the Rotunda at sunrise, where it remained in a serene display up until the eve of his burial on Thursday.

It was announced that the following Thursday at 11 o'clock, President Nixon would give his eloquence to eulogize a life—a life that had irrevocably molded the Federal Bureau of Investigation. The air was filled with reverence and recollection. Hoover's unwavering attitude had left his mark on the very structure of the organization he had led; the agency was effective, though controversial, yet, impervious to corruption, and unwavering in its goals.

When the mortal coil let go, tremors echoed through the executive offices. A discussion that was as deep as it was unavoidable was sparked by Hoover's departure.

For years before this time, the agency's focal areas had come under criticism from the left of the political spectrum for being too passionate in their pursuit of radicals and purported subversives while being too soft in their confrontation with organized crime and white-collar offenders. The direction that the agency should take was highlighted by this separation.

It was rumored that President Nixon's pick of a successor would be a diplomatic dance, one that could only be done once the results of the November election were finalized. This developing story became more complicated due to the continuing Senate discussion over Mr. Kleindienst's confirmation. In the middle of everything, it became clear that someone else would assume interim directorship. At the age of 71, Clyde A. Tolson, the stalwart assistant director of the FBI, was informed by the winds of change that he would not be considered for the position of acting director. This announcement served as a subtle reminder that the leadership legacy had then turned its attention to other horizons.

CHAPTER FIVE

CONCLUSION

The mysterious persona of J. Edgar Hoover emerges as a mosaic of authority and ambiguity in the complicated fabric of American history. Hoover, a pioneering architect of the Federal Bureau of Investigation (FBI), left behind an enduring testament to the unwavering pursuit, unwavering discipline, and an insatiable ambition for perfection in law enforcement.

Hoover's life unfolded inside the halls of political power from his modest beginnings in the arms of a family with strong government ties, his boyhood footsteps resonating close to Capitol Hill's center. For him, a childhood immersed in public service not only fostered an unflinching loyalty to the government's cause but also served as the foundation for his identity, which would influence the course of his whole life.

Hoover's firm hold transformed the FBI into his own mirror as he assumed control of the organization. Swift, tenacious, and unwavering, he promoted forensic science and the academic study of law enforcement, endowing scholarships and motivating generations of aspirants to steadfastly stand at the nexus of justice and truth.

Shadows always appear where brightness sheds its radiance, however. Hoover came dangerously near to going too far in his obsessive pursuit of order. His COINTELPRO endeavors tainted his legacy, shedding a depressing light on the thin line separating watchful patriotism from the possible erasure of morality for the sake of social balance. The intricate account of his connection with Clyde Tolson, which is laced with hints of a deep affinity, loyalty, and maybe even passion, adds mystery to his tale and prompts questions that linger on the edges of time.

J. Edgar Hoover continues to be a mystery in the stillness of remembrance—a physical manifestation of the complex dance between the need for order and the unrelenting pursuit of justice. His legacy raises important questions on the complexities of leadership, the strength of authority, and the persistent desire to build a society on the pillars of truth and integrity.

Nonetheless, it is clear by examining the story of J. Edgar Hoover's life that he made extraordinary contributions to the development of the Federal Bureau of Investigation and the current state of law enforcement. Hoover turned a young organization into a hub of investigative expertise by unyielding resolve and imaginative leadership, establishing in it ideals of discipline, order, and the quest for perfection. He oversaw the FBI's development into an organization that upheld the principles of justice and the search for the truth.

Despite the conflicts and arguments that dogged his tenure, Hoover's legacy is one that is complex. While his methods and choices may come under scrutiny, it's important to recognize the substantial contributions he made to preventing crime, promoting scientific research, and maintaining national security in turbulent times. His unrelenting commitment to these objectives contributed to laying the groundwork for contemporary law enforcement organizations.

The life of J. Edgar Hoover is a witness to the complex interactions. His influence on the development of law enforcement is still evident, notwithstanding the complications that surround his name. His successes and the lessons learned from the story of leadership are best understood within this larger perspective, which compels us to reflect on the complicated legacy of a man who made an enduring impression on the annals of history. He might not have been a perfect man, but

he was passionate with good intentions.

Printed in Great Britain
by Amazon